This book belongs to

_____

This edition published by Parragon Books Ltd in 2017

Parragon Books Ltd
Chartist House
15–17 Trim Street
Bath BA1 1HA, UK
www.parragon.com

Illustrated by: Livia Coloji
Reading consultant: Geraldine Taylor

ISBN 978-1-4748-6309-4

Printed in China

FIRST READERS

The Ugly Duckling

PaRragon

Bath · New York · Cologne · Melbourne · Delhi
Hong Kong · Shenzhen · Singapore

Five steps for enjoyable reading

Traditional stories and fairy tales are
a great way to begin reading practice.
The stories and characters are familiar
and lively. Follow the steps below to
help your child become a confident
and independent reader.

Step 1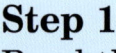
Read the story
aloud to your
child. Run your
finger under the
words as you read.

One day, six fluffy yellow ducklings
hatched from their eggs. Mother Duck
was very happy.
   "Cheep, cheep!"
the ducklings called
to their mother.

8

Step 2
Look at the
pictures and
talk about what
is happening.

Step 3
Read the simple text on the right-hand page
together. When reading, some words come
up again and again, such as **the**, **to** or **and**.
Your child will quickly learn to recognize
these high-frequency words by sight.

But there was one big egg left
the nest.

9

Step 4
When your
child is ready,
encourage them
to read the simple
lines on their own.

Step 5
Help your child to complete the
puzzles at the back of the book.

One day, six fluffy yellow ducklings
hatched from their eggs. Mother Duck
was very happy.
"Cheep, cheep!"
the ducklings called
to their mother.

But there was one big egg left
in the nest.

At last, the big egg cracked open.
Out popped a funny grey duckling
with big black feet and a big black
beak. The other ducks crowded
around to look with Mother Duck.

"It does not look like a
duckling," they said.

Mother Duck gathered up her fluffy yellow ducklings and her funny grey duckling.

"Follow me," she said. She led them through the farmyard.

All the animals stopped to stare at the funny grey duckling.

The animals made fun of him.

13

When they got to the pond, Mother Duck and the fluffy yellow ducklings swam off. The funny grey duckling was left behind.

"Go away," said the goose. "You are ugly."

"You are not one of us,"
she said.

The funny grey duckling went back to the barn. But the fluffy yellow ducklings wouldn't play with him.

"Go away," they said. "You are not like us. You don't belong here."

The little duckling was very sad.
He ran away.

The funny grey duckling walked for miles until he came to a cottage. A little old woman gave him some corn and milk.

"Go away!" said the hen. "You are eating all my grain."

"Go away!" said the cat. "You are drinking all my milk."

"And don't come back," said the cat and the hen.

19

The funny grey duckling went back to the pond. But winter was coming and the pond was turning to ice.

The funny grey duckling was cold and hungry. He saw some swans fly over the pond.

"I wish I could fly up in the sky with the swans," he thought.

The swans did not see him.
They flew far away.

At last, winter turned to spring. The fluffy yellow ducklings came back to the pond. But they had grown up. Now, they were ducks. They saw the ugly grey duckling. But he had grown up too. He was not a duck at all.

"If I am not a duck, what am I?"
he asked.

The ugly duckling looked down into the water and saw his reflection.
"I look just like a swan!"
he said, surprised.

"I am a swan!" he shouted with joy.

Just then, the swans flew over and landed on the pond.

"Hello," said one of the swans. "Do you want to come with us?"

The ugly duckling – now a fine swan – was so happy!

He flew away with the other swans.

Puzzle time!

Which two words rhyme?

sad   can   fun   run   far

Which word does not match the picture?

black
green
grey

Which words match the picture?

swan
swim
swap

Who ran away?

duckling
hen
cat

Which sentence is right?

I wish I could fly.
I wish I were a fly.